The North East

Edited By Brixie Payne

First published in Great Britain in 2019 by:

Young Writers
Remus House
Coltsfoot Drive
Peterborough
PE2 9BF
Telephone: 01733 890066
Website: www.youngwriters.co.uk

Foreword

Dear Reader,

Are you ready to explore the wonderful delights of poetry?

Young Writers' *Poetry Patrol* gang set out to encourage and ignite the imaginations of 5-7 year-olds as they took their first steps into the magical world of poetry. With **Riddling Rabbit**, **Acrostic Croc** and **Sensory Skunk** on hand to help, children were invited to write an acrostic, sense poem or riddle on any theme, from people to places, animals to objects, food to seasons. *Poetry Patrol* is also a great way to introduce children to the use of poetic expression, including onomatopoeia and similes, repetition and metaphors, acting as stepping stones for their future poetic journey.

All of us here at Young Writers believe in the importance of inspiring young children to produce creative writing, including poetry, and we feel that seeing their own poem in print will keep that creative spirit burning brightly and proudly.

We hope you enjoy reading this wonderful collection as much as we enjoyed reading all the entries.

Contents

St Catherine's RC Primary School, Sandyford

Anna Fedorova (5)	60
Max Askwith (5)	61
Max Robertson (5)	62
Ahmad Saleh Mohamed (5)	63
Sadie Delanoy (5)	64

St Patrick's RC Primary School, Fairfield

Freddy Bonner (6)	65
Joseph Louis Bakewell (6)	66
Isabelle Dorothy Christine Davison (6)	68
Rome Kilpatrick (6)	70
Shari Grace Mcgregor (6)	72
Henry Chen (6)	74
Freya May Francis (6)	75
Anya Paige Freeman (6), Elliott Atkins & Sienna Constance Muwonge (7)	76
Kai Johnson (6)	77
Toby Mamello Jones (6)	78
Tommy Parker-Wood (6)	79
James Saint (6)	80
Eliza Matilda Herrity (6)	81
Samuel Russell (6)	82
Joe (7)	83

Wellgate Primary School, Mapplewell

Amelia Yasmin Wilson (6)	84
Olivia Josie Elizabeth Pidcock (7)	85
Ava Flintham (6)	86
Samuel Alexander Higgs (6)	87
Poppy B (6)	88
Elisia C (5)	89
Grace G (6)	90
Poppy N (6)	91
Lucas Jonathan Underwood-Varley (6)	92
Caitlin N (6)	93

Isaac M (6)	94
Sophi Mai Deakin (7)	95
Jude Elijah Burd (5)	96
Thea Hartshorne (5)	97
Ethan Robert Wealthall (6)	98
Tamara B (7)	99
Maggie Be (5)	100
Charlie Ewan M D (6)	101
Betsy Lea (6)	102
Noah Michael Taylor (6)	103
Harris C (6)	104
Gabriella M (5)	105
Sam S (6)	106
Sophie E (6)	107
Matilda Rose Hope (5)	108
Riley M (6)	109
Harry Flintham (6)	110
Louie F (6)	111
Tiana S (5)	112
Charlie Exley (6)	113
Alanis King (5)	114
Violet Valentine Jackson (6)	115
Layla Louise Kaye (6)	116
Ethan Ogley (6)	117
Archie J Chapman stott (6)	118
Rosie B (5)	119
Lewis Cummings (5)	120
Luca F Lazzarano (5)	121
Brooke Carolyne Seward (6)	122
Archie Daniel Mallinder (5)	123
Brooklyn B (5)	124
Amelia Rachel Galloway (6)	125
Jack C (6)	126
Charlotte Buckle (5)	127
Chloe Anna Hague (6)	128
Ollie Beau Rawson (5)	129
Daisy Olivia M (6)	130
Robert W (5)	131
Owen S (6)	132
Daisy Mary Knight (5)	133
Maisie G (5)	134
Autumn M (5)	135
Tommy T (6)	136

Kian S (5)	137
Zain C (5)	138
Charlie H (5)	139
John S (5)	140
Emily S (6)	141
Ashton O (7)	142
Riley F (6)	143
James V (5)	144
Harry Jay Thomas (5)	145
Harri Ball (6)	146
Lily Littledyke (5)	147
Oliver J (5)	148
Oscar Lumb (5)	149
Noah E (5)	150

The Poems

RIDDLIN' RABBIT

SENSORY SKUNK

ACROSTIC CROC

What Am I?

I have big teeth.
I have fire inside.
I have a long tail.
I eat chocolate cake.
I eat people.
I have blue spikes.
My body is scaly.
What am I?

Answer: A dragon.

Harley Moore (5)
Grindon Hall Christian School, Nookside

What Am I?

I can swim.
I love fish.
I live on an ice cube forever and ever,
it is cold.
I have loads of brothers and sisters
and a mam and dad.
What am I?

Answer: A penguin.

Eden Grace Ranton (5)
Grindon Hall Christian School, Nookside

What Am I?

I have teeth.
I have big feet.
I have a bed.
I have big eyes.
I have big legs.
I jump.
I have a furry tail.
What am I?

Answer: A rabbit.

Alissia Winter (5)

Grindon Hall Christian School, Nookside

What Am I?

I can fly.
I have a horn.
I have four legs.
I dance everywhere.
I have a white tummy.
What am I?

Answer: A unicorn.

Cecilia Cuthbertson (5)

Grindon Hall Christian School, Nookside

What Am I?

I have a black head.
I have eight legs.
I have furry legs.
What am I?

Answer: A caterpillar.

Cornelia Dmytrowska (5)
Grindon Hall Christian School, Nookside

What Am I?

I bounce everywhere.
I jump really high.
I eat carrots.
What am I?

Answer: A bunny rabbit.

Max Gallant (6)
Grindon Hall Christian School, Nookside

What Am I?

I have long legs.
I like apples.
I run fast.
I am grey.
What am I?

Answer: A pony.

Summer Bell (6)
Grindon Hall Christian School, Nookside

What Am I?

I have grey fur.
I nibble carrots.
I have four legs.
What am I?

Answer: A bunny rabbit.

Lucy Davison (6)
Grindon Hall Christian School, Nookside

What Am I?

I have big wings.
I have a long neck.
I have four legs.
What am I?

Answer: A dragon.

TJ Bainbridge (5)
Grindon Hall Christian School, Nookside

What Am I?

I have four legs.
I nibble carrots.
I hop.
What am I?

Answer: A bunny rabbit.

Hugo Lo (5)
Grindon Hall Christian School, Nookside

Football Is Here!

F ast, fast down the pitch.

O h no, a foul! Or has he got a stitch?

O n we run to the other end -

T oo many players ready to defend.

B rilliant, finally a chance to shoot,

A really loud thud as the ball hits the boot.

L ook, it's going... but bounces off the pole,

L et's get a rebound - time for a goal!

James Craven (6)

Levendale Primary School, Yarm

Bonfire Night

Bonfire Night smells like
burning wood and hot dogs.
I can see bright colourful fireworks
in the dark sky.
All around me fireworks whizz,
whoosh and bang.
The loud noises fill my cold ears.
It is cold outside but I feel cosy
in my scarf and gloves.
Bonfire Night is a special time of the year.

Evie Rathmell (6)
Levendale Primary School, Yarm

Pokémon Go!

P ikachu was the first one found

O nyx can dig underground

K adabra holds a silver spoon

E kans slithers around the room

M uk is stinky in a fight

O ddish only comes out at night

N inetales makes the others rest.

(I like Charizard X the best).

Isaac Harris (6)

Levendale Primary School, Yarm

My Special Pet

H appy is how I feel when I play with her

A lways running and climbing around

M y daddy and my mummy clean her cage

S he is a big sleeper

T iny claws and soft, fluffy fur

E ating quickly and storing food in her chubby cheeks

R ebecca is her name.

George Hannaway (6)
Levendale Primary School, Yarm

A Halloween Riddle

I have a big, pointy hat.
My favourite colour is black.
I cackle when I am happy.
I have my own black cat.
I have a green wart on my nose.
I am sometimes scary.
I make potions in my cauldron.
I fly on a broomstick.
What am I?

Answer: A witch.

Emily Makepeace (6)
Levendale Primary School, Yarm

White Beauty

I am very old.
I am always cold with a white face.
I am very strong.
People like to climb on my head.
Not everyone can do it though.
I am always beautiful.
I am the tallest in the world.
I live in Nepal.
What am I?

Answer: Mount Everest.

Sahana Karthikeyan (6)
Levendale Primary School, Yarm

Spooky

I am bony, I don't eat at all.
I scare people at Halloween.
I have ribs and a skull.
I have no brain, I am not clever.
I am good at scaring people.
I have no eyes that is why I am spooky.
What am I?

Answer: A skeleton.

Jessica Elder (6)
Levendale Primary School, Yarm

What Am I?

I love carrots,
But I am not a parrot.
I love jumping over logs,
But I am not a frog.
I am not as big as a whale,
Nor as slow as a snail.
You can ride on me,
If you give me a pea.
What am I?

Answer: A horse.

Sofia Antonia Roberts-Cano (6)
Levendale Primary School, Yarm

Who Am I?

I am part of three superheroes
Who save the world.
I am the boss.
My real name is Tony Stark.
I wear a suit of armour.
I shoot energy beams.
Hulk and Wasp are in my amazing team.
Who am I?

Answer: Iron Man.

Aden Hutton (6)
Levendale Primary School, Yarm

What Am I?

I twirl brightly.
You put me up twelve days
Before my special day.
I am green and spiky.
I have space for a fairy on top of me.
You decorate me how you want to.
What am I?

Answer: A Christmas tree.

Imogen Rowney (6)
Levendale Primary School, Yarm

Dolls

Dolls live in big houses.
Dolls wear pretty dresses.
Dolls wear high heels.
Dolls have pretty bedrooms.
Dolls have pink lips.
I pretend to play with my doll kitchen.
Dolls are fun for little girls to play with.

Isabella Coakley (6)

Levendale Primary School, Yarm

Bedtime

Sometimes at night, I just can't sleep,
I lie in bed counting sheep,
I shout downstairs
and tell Mum I am awake,
I then get back in bed
and try again to sleep,
Suddenly, it's morning and I am yawning.

Toby Mellor (6)
Levendale Primary School, Yarm

My Baby Sister Anna

Anna smells like pretty flowers.
Anna looks like a little angel.
Anna feels fluffy like a unicorn.
Anna is a noisy chatterbox.
Anna reminds me of a cute teddy.
Anna is my baby sister and I love her.

Sophie Ellis (6)
Levendale Primary School, Yarm

Rabbit

R abbit is my friend
A rabbit bounces to the funky beat
B rown fur
B ig ears
I s hungry because it likes carrots
T akes me to bed every night. Goodnight.

Orla Davis (6)
Levendale Primary School, Yarm

An Animal Riddle

I am a family pet.
I have four legs.
I am furry and I have whiskers.
I like to catch mice.
I have sharp claws
And I make a purring sound.
What am I?

Answer: A cat.

Freya Murphy (6)
Levendale Primary School, Yarm

Night Visitor

I have spikes and fur in-between.
I like to live in leaves.
I have a button nose.
I come out at night.
I am scared if I roll into a ball.
What am I?

Answer: A hedgehog.

Luca Cunningham (6)

Levendale Primary School, Yarm

A Sport

There are eleven players on each team.
You can play on the AstroTurf.
You win by scoring lots of goals.
You only play with hands and feet.
What is it?

Answer: Football.

Thomas Grant Mateos (6)
Levendale Primary School, Yarm

My Favourite Sport

It makes me sweat.
I play it every Wednesday.
I play in a team.
I have a red kit.
I play on the grass.
I score goals.
What is it?

Answer: Football.

Oliver Buxton (6)
Levendale Primary School, Yarm

Alfie Dog

D aft dog chasing his tail

O pening all of our mail

G o for a walk and Mummy talks

S nuggle and cuddle, me and my dog Alfie.

Imogen Rose Stephen (6)

Levendale Primary School, Yarm

My Friend, Bobby The Dog

Bobby smells different to me.
Bobby tastes my fingers.
Bobby looks fluffy.
Bobby feels soft and warm.
Bobby sounds loud when he barks.

Ruby Pinder (6)

Levendale Primary School, Yarm

The Gingerbread Man

I have a gingerbread man called Sam,
My grandma is called Pam,
I have a rabbit called Bam-Bam,
They all love eating jam.

Lydia Honeyman-Perry (6)
Levendale Primary School, Yarm

Tasty Food

Amazing apples
Blue berries
Cold carrots
Dumpy dumplings
Cracky crackers
Yummy yoghurt
Quiet quiche
Juicy juice.

Harrison Hindmarch (7)
Nettlesworth Primary School, Nettlesworth

Tasty Food

Amazing apples
Melty marshmallows
Delicious doughnuts
Flappy fish
Icy ice cream
Crunchy crackers.

Robyn Sarah Snowball (6)

Nettlesworth Primary School, Nettlesworth

Tasty Food

Creamy cream
Delicious doughnuts
Fierce fish
Amazing apples
Orange oranges
Flappy flapjacks.

Lucas Howard (6)
Nettlesworth Primary School, Nettlesworth

Tasty Food

I have lots of delicious food in my house like:
Delicious doughnuts
Ruby raspberries
Flappy fish
Kind kiwis
Playful peas
Melty marshmallows
Boiling bananas
Crunchy carrots.

Isla Rose Rutherford (6)
Nettlesworth Primary School, Nettlesworth

Tasty Food

Delicious doughnuts
Beautiful blueberries
Sour lemons
Beautiful bananas
Sweet strawberries.

Jake Hunter Black (6)
Nettlesworth Primary School, Nettlesworth

Dinosaur

D inosaur Praim

I s a diplodocus

N one of his friends can fly

O n a Sunday

S cary

A nimals

U nder

R ooftops.

Charlie John Whittington (5)

Nettlesworth Primary School, Nettlesworth

Tasty Food

Floppy fish fountain
Delicious doughnut disaster
Poopy peas please
Igloo ice cream.

Charlie Jack Rendall (5)
Nettlesworth Primary School, Nettlesworth

Lovely Hearts

D inosaur Chaz
I s fierce
N ext
O n the
S lide
A round the
U nicorns
R ain.

Farren Davison (5)
Nettlesworth Primary School, Nettlesworth

Dinosaur

D inosaur

I n a

N ut tree

O mnivore

S earching for

A pples

U nder

R ipe.

Millie Joyce Barron (5)
Nettlesworth Primary School, Nettlesworth

Dino

D inosaur Sophia has a brother

I n his room, he has a cot

N ext, he has a dummy

O n a night, he cries for his dummy.

Sophia Logan (6)
Nettlesworth Primary School, Nettlesworth

Tasty Food

Delicious doughnuts
Prickly pineapple
Amazing apples
Rosy raspberry
Hairy hot dog
Melty marshmallows
Orange orange.

Amelia Rose Lee (6)
Nettlesworth Primary School, Nettlesworth

Dino

D inosaur George is as fast as lightning
I n and out of the obstacles
N ight-time, he sleeps
O n a bed.

George Corrigan (5)

Nettlesworth Primary School, Nettlesworth

Dino

D inosaur Evie has a doll

I n her room, is a doll's house

N ight, she flies

O utside.

Evie Thompson (6)
Nettlesworth Primary School, Nettlesworth

Tasty Food

Toilet tomato
Orange orange
Dumpy doughnut
Hairy hot dog
Wet water
Poopy peas
Crunchy carrots.

Alfie Harle (6)
Nettlesworth Primary School, Nettlesworth

Tasty Food

Crunchy carrots
Delicious doughnuts
Amazing apples
Super strawberries
Icy ice lollies.

Pearl White-Hunt (6)

Nettlesworth Primary School, Nettlesworth

Tasty Food

Delicious doughnuts
Flappy fish
Lemony lemons
Creamy cream
Poppy peas.

Jenson Aspinall (6)
Nettlesworth Primary School, Nettlesworth

Tasty Food

Amazing apples.
Enormous eggs.
Delicious doughnuts.
Juicy juice.

Marcus John Stephenson (7)
Nettlesworth Primary School, Nettlesworth

Dinosaur Dad

D eadly
I ndoraptor
N aughty
O range.

Jacob Howard (4)

Nettlesworth Primary School, Nettlesworth

Hungry Dino

D eadly
I ntelligent
N ice
O range.

Erica Anne Headlam (4)
Nettlesworth Primary School, Nettlesworth

T-Rex

D eadly
I nside
N ice
O pen mouth.

Connie Louise Hadwin (4)

Nettlesworth Primary School, Nettlesworth

Dinosaur

D inosaur
I nside
N ice
O livia.

Olivia Smith (4)
Nettlesworth Primary School, Nettlesworth

Deadly Dino

D eadly

I ntelligent

N est

O dd.

Sam Ellis Jamieson (5)

Nettlesworth Primary School, Nettlesworth

Tasty Food

Orange oranges
Perfect plums
Appley apples
Juicy juice.

Praim Bassi (6)

Nettlesworth Primary School, Nettlesworth

Dino Danny

D eadly

I ndoraptor

N est

O dd.

Ryan Jamie Elliott (6)

Nettlesworth Primary School, Nettlesworth

Tasty Food

Perfect plum
Icy ice cream
Orange orange
Lovely lemon.

Lucie Ella Punshon (5)
Nettlesworth Primary School, Nettlesworth

T-Rex

D inosaur

I n

N asty

O utback.

Joshua James Burnip (5)
Nettlesworth Primary School, Nettlesworth

Tasty Food

Amazing apples
Sweets
Yummy eggs
Orange oranges.

Amelia Capja (7)
Nettlesworth Primary School, Nettlesworth

Tasty Food

Crunchy carrots
Amazing apples
Lovely lettuce.

Matthew Boden (5)

Nettlesworth Primary School, Nettlesworth

What Am I?

I am juicy.
I can be purple.
I can be green.
My juice is good and sweet.
Sometimes I am big or I can be small.
I come in a bunch.
I am healthy for your body.
What am I?

Answer: A grape.

Anna Fedorova (5)
St Catherine's RC Primary School, Sandyford

What Am I?

I am big.
I have sharp teeth.
I have sharp claws.
I eat people.
I am extinct.
I am green.
I have a big mouth.
I am scary.
I roar.
I run fast.
What am I?

Answer: A T-rex.

Max Askwith (5)
St Catherine's RC Primary School, Sandyford

What Am I?

I am as fast as the speed of light.
I use my big brown wings to glide.
I have a pointy yellow peak.
I live up high in the mountains.
What am I?

Answer: A peregrine falcon.

Max Robertson (5)
St Catherine's RC Primary School, Sandyford

What Am I?

I am small.
I am fluffy.
Cats scare me.
I like to eat cheese.
I have a tail.
I squeak.
What am I?

Answer: A mouse.

Ahmad Saleh Mohamed (5)
St Catherine's RC Primary School, Sandyford

What Am I?

I talk funny.
My skin is yellow.
I am in a type of movie.
What am I?

Answer: A Minion.

Sadie Delanoy (5)
St Catherine's RC Primary School, Sandyford

World War I

W ounded soldiers dead on the floor

O range sky with airships

R ed moon in the sky and soldiers running

L eading soldiers through cannons exploding

D ark moon and dead men on the floor

W arships coming and aeroplanes dropping bombs, sad for dead people

A ir foggy with smoke

R ed poppies growing

1 914 - 1918

Freddy Bonner (6)

St Patrick's RC Primary School, Fairfield

Poppies To Help Remember

P oppies grow as the soldiers die
O verhead, the enemies are there
P eople die as the war goes on
P eople die with fear
I will remember the soldiers that died
E nemies are running with fear
S ome people are on a suicide mission!

T hanks to the soldiers, we are alive
O verhead, the planes are in the sky

H ell is here, what to do?
E verybody is shooting and there are more
deaths of men
L ots of bombs are dropping from the sky
P eople are scared, people are dead

R emember the soldiers in the war

E verybody in the trenches is frightened

M ore people begin to die

E veryone is panicking, who has the win?

M ore tanks are driving

B e strong and helpful

E verybody is screaming in pain

R emember the men who saved our lives.

Joseph Louis Bakewell (6)
St Patrick's RC Primary School, Fairfield

World War I

P eople went out with hope

O nly brave soldiers went out to war

P eople thought everyone was going to be fine

P eople shot the enemy during the war

I n the sky, flew aeroplanes shooting bombs

E normous guns were shooting fire

S oldiers died during the war

T rees were shot, things were shot

O ther animals were shot too

H elp people to remember the war

E nemies were killed, grass was burnt

L ots of people were sad

P oppies grew where they lay

R emember soldiers who died

E nemies are now gone

M ore and more people get poppies now

E at as much food as they could

M ore people like poppies

B ut still now, you get fights

E agles flew in the sky and feathers came down

R abbits ran as they saw guns.

Isabelle Dorothy Christine Davison (6)

St Patrick's RC Primary School, Fairfield

World War I

P oppies grew as the enemies died

O nce there was a battle, it was called a war

P oor time it was

P eople began to die

I t was sad

E nemies died as aeroplanes flew

S oldiers died in the past

T oday, we continue to remember

O nce there was a battle, it started in 1914

H elp to remember

E veryone in the battle

L ead the way to the poppies

P eople go and pick the poppies

R emember poppies

E veryone died except sixteen people

M ade loads of money

E ach gun shot people

M ay we always remember the people who died

B ombs exploded

E ven today we still remember

R emember the people who died.

Rome Kilpatrick (6)

St Patrick's RC Primary School, Fairfield

One Hundred Years

O n the day, bullets flew across the sky

N ot many soldiers did survive the war

E veryone looked at the bullets in the sky

H ungry soldiers getting defeated in the war

U sed guns to defeat the enemies in the tanks

N ot any food to eat in the war

D efeated enemies to stay safe

R an from the bullets flying through the air

E ven the bravest died in the war

D ied in the war flying aeroplanes

Y ears ago, people died in the war to keep us safe

E very day, we feel safer

A s the days got better, more poppies grew

R ose the aeroplanes to be safe

S afe people helped the war people.

Shari Grace Mcgregor (6)

St Patrick's RC Primary School, Fairfield

World War I

W ounded soldiers everywhere
O range sky as they die
R ockets drop bombs into their hearts
L eading men to fight
D ying soldiers as they fight

W alking around ready to shoot
A s the poppies grow, people die
R eady to shoot as the soldiers die

1 914 - 1918.

Henry Chen (6)
St Patrick's RC Primary School, Fairfield

World War I

W ounded soldiers everywhere
O range sky as they died
R unning with fear
L eading men to fight
D ripping blood all over

W alking wounded, many people died
A s the poppies grew, people died
R emember always

1 914 - 1918.

Freya May Francis (6)

St Patrick's RC Primary School, Fairfield

World War I

W ounded soldiers everywhere

O range sky as they died

R unning with fear

L eading men to fight

D ripping blood all over

W alking wounded

A s the poppies grew, people died

R emember always

1 914 - 1918.

Anya Paige Freeman (6), Elliott Atkins & Sienna Constance Muwonge (7)
St Patrick's RC Primary School, Fairfield

Poppies

P oppies grew longer than roses
O n jets, there were guns firing
P eople ran away from guns
P eople hid from gunshots and ran
I t was a danger for people
E veryone was running for their lives
S cared at night when there were bombs.

Kai Johnson (6)
St Patrick's RC Primary School, Fairfield

World War I

W ar felt so sad and bad

O range sky so smoky

R un oh run, bombs!

L and ships firing shells

D ropping bombs was terrible

W ounded soldiers running

A s poppies grew, people died

R unning fast to bomb shelters.

Toby Mamello Jones (6)

St Patrick's RC Primary School, Fairfield

Poppies

P eople began to die

O nly brave soldiers decided to fight

P oppies replaced the soldiers

P oppies were everywhere when everyone was dead

I remember the soldiers

E veryone died

S adly when the war ended, everyone was dead.

Tommy Parker-Wood (6)

St Patrick's RC Primary School, Fairfield

World War One

W ounded soldiers died

O range sky as they died

R unning with fear

L oud explosives

D ripping blood

W alking in the war

A s the poppies grew, people died

R emember always

1 914 - 1918.

James Saint (6)

St Patrick's RC Primary School, Fairfield

World War I

W ounded soldiers everywhere
O range sky as they died
R unning with fear
L eading men to fight
D ripping blood all over

W alking wounded
A s the poppies grew, people died
R emember always.

Eliza Matilda Herrity (6)
St Patrick's RC Primary School, Fairfield

Poppies

P oppies grew when soldiers died

O ne soldier was strong

P oor people had to fight

P oppies grew where soldiers died

I can help remember the soldiers

E veryone was fighting

S ome people helped to fight.

Samuel Russell (6)

St Patrick's RC Primary School, Fairfield

Poppies

P eople died in the war
O ne poppy stood as the special one
P oppies were special for everyone
P oor people died
I n the war
E veryone unfortunately died but poppies grew
S till we remember them.

Joe (7)
St Patrick's RC Primary School, Fairfield

Halloween Horrors

Halloween feels like creepy furry spiders are crawling onto your costume when you are getting ready to go trick or treating at your friend's house.

When you get to the scary wicked witch's house, you might get terrible nightmares! Halloween sounds like zombies pushing their way out from the red blood-like graveyards.

Halloween smells like chocolate and little Coca-Cola Haribos.

When it's Halloween and you go back home, you can taste the sweet sweets and lovely love heart cookies.

You wander around the scary horrid world of monsters.

Make sure you don't eat too many sweeties!

Amelia Yasmin Wilson (6)

Wellgate Primary School, Mapplewell

Halloween

Halloween looks like a spooky frightful
pumpkin.
How scary it is!
Halloween looks like a burning pumpkin lid.
Halloween smells like a roasting pumpkin.
Halloween smells like sugary toffee.
Halloween feels like a sticky pumpkin.
Halloween feels like a scrunchy pumpkin.
Halloween tastes like green lollies.
Halloween tastes like gummy sweets.
Halloween sounds like ghosts howling.
Halloween sounds like wicked witches
cackling as they stir their green bubbly
potion.

Olivia Josie Elizabeth Pidcock (7)

Wellgate Primary School, Mapplewell

Halloween

Halloween looks like green ugly witches
flying through the dark sky.
Halloween looks like creepy ugly goblins
digging their way out of a graveyard.
Halloween smells like
gooey, sticky caramel apples.
Halloween smells like
some delicious pumpkins.
Halloween feels like
squishy flavoured candy.
Halloween tastes like mouthwatering
chocolate in your basket.

Ava Flintham (6)

Wellgate Primary School, Mapplewell

Halloween

Halloween looks like a zombie climbing out
of a haunted graveyard.
Halloween smells like a few grey
pumpkin lids.
Halloween feels like a sticky toffee apple.
Halloween tastes like
some scrumptious candy.
Halloween sounds like
rattling skeleton bones.
Halloween reminds me of witches
casting spells.

Samuel Alexander Higgs (6)
Wellgate Primary School, Mapplewell

Halloween

Halloween looks like some evil vampires sucking everyone's blood.
Halloween smells like some burning pumpkin lids.
Halloween tastes like some squishy sweets.
Halloween feels like some smooth shiny doorbells.
Halloween sounds like some screaming kids getting scared by all the gruesome costumes.
Halloween reminds me of some dark nights and lots of black bats.

Poppy B (6)

Wellgate Primary School, Mapplewell

Autumn

Autumn smells of sweet, sticky
marshmallows on the toasty fire.
Autumn tastes like sweet,
crisp toffee apples.
Autumn looks like leaves falling down
so they make a carpet.
Autumn feels warm
with clothes keeping you warm.
Autumn sounds like trees whistling.
Autumn reminds me of playing.

Elisia C (5)
Wellgate Primary School, Mapplewell

Halloween

Halloween looks like lots of orange, sticky, boiling hot, glowing pumpkins.
Halloween feels very scary because you can see very scary costumes.
Halloween smells very smoky
because of the pumpkins.
Halloween tastes sticky and squishy.
Halloween sounds like spooky screams.
Sometimes they can be scary cackles.
Halloween is very scary.

Grace G (6)

Wellgate Primary School, Mapplewell

Halloween Horrors

Halloween smells like some delicious, yummy, jubbly sweets that children like to collect around the scary village.
Halloween looks like many fluffy spiders that are crawling on gravestones making webs all over.
Halloween tastes like a disgusting witch's potion in a cauldron with slimy frogs and a broomstick that crunches when you stir the bubbly mess.
Halloween feels like many demons are watching your every move.

Poppy N (6)
Wellgate Primary School, Mapplewell

Halloween

Halloween looks like a scary haunted house.
Halloween smells like tasty,
mouthwatering sweets.
Halloween feels like squishy pumpkins.
Halloween tastes like scary pumpkins.
Halloween tastes like
mouthwatering sweets.
Halloween sounds like bats
flapping their wings.

Lucas Jonathan Underwood-Varley (6)

Wellgate Primary School, Mapplewell

Halloween

Halloween looks like there are lots of
spooky skeletons crawling out of the
ground.
Witches cackle loudly.
Halloween smells like sticky, sweet,
sugary sweets.
Halloween tastes like sweet spiders,
cackling witches and sweet candy apples.
Halloween sounds like skeletons
rattling their bones.

Caitlin N (6)

Wellgate Primary School, Mapplewell

Halloween

Halloween looks like scary invisible ghosts.
Halloween sounds like a knight that has red
armour and a scary voice.
Halloween tastes like sour, sugary,
sticky candy.
Halloween sounds like brown fluffy bats.
Halloween looks like jack-o'-lanterns.
Halloween looks like rattling skeletons
crawling out of dirty graves.
Halloween feels like green
poisonous zombies.
Halloween sounds like spiders making white
sticky webs.

Isaac M (6)

Wellgate Primary School, Mapplewell

Trick Or Treat

Halloween smells like pumpkin pie that is so yummy and smells like sweets as well.
Halloween sounds like a spooky owl cooing in the darkness.
Halloween feels like a scary cobweb that many spiders made.
Halloween tastes like some sticky nice sweets.
Halloween looks like many furry spiders creeping through the cracks in people's floors.

Sophi Mai Deakin (7)

Wellgate Primary School, Mapplewell

Autumn

Autumn smells of roasted marshmallows
on the fire.
Autumn tastes like sweet
toffee apples crunching.
Autumn looks like colourful leaves
falling to the ground.
Autumn feels like soft leaves.
Autumn sounds like tweeting birds
in their nests.

Jude Elijah Burd (5)

Wellgate Primary School, Mapplewell

Autumn

Autumn smells of yellow honey
and clear wind.
Autumn tastes like yummy chocolate
and vanilla ice cream.
Autumn looks like a raspberry lolly.
Autumn feels like clear wind.
Autumn sounds like wind in the sky.
Autumn reminds me of feeling warm.

Thea Hartshorne (5)
Wellgate Primary School, Mapplewell

Halloween

Halloween looks like some red devils.
Halloween smells like scary zombies coming
out of the ground.
Can you see the spooky trees swaying?
Halloween feels like some sticky candy!
Halloween sounds like haunted houses.
Halloween tastes like sweets and candy.

Ethan Robert Wealthall (6)
Wellgate Primary School, Mapplewell

Halloween

Halloween looks like green zombies breaking into houses.
Halloween smells like lots of mouthwatering sugary candy.
Halloween feels like invisible floating ghosts.
Halloween tastes like loads of nice scrumptious sweets.
Halloween sounds like lots of ugly green goblins coming our way.

Tamara B (7)

Wellgate Primary School, Mapplewell

Autumn

Autumn smells of yummy hot food
cooking in the kitchen.
Autumn tastes like yummy chocolate cake
in my belly.
Autumn looks fun - the grass is getting long
and the leaves are falling down.
Autumn feels cold and wet and windy.
Autumn sounds like birds tweeting
and wolves howling.
Autumn reminds me of summer ending,
stories and Bonfire Night.

Maggie Be (5)
Wellgate Primary School, Mapplewell

Trick Or Treat

Halloween looks fun because you can collect yummy sweets.
Halloween smells like sweets.
Halloween feels like there is someone behind me on the street.
Halloween tastes of sticky, yummy, tasty sweets and pumpkin pie.
Halloween looks like I'm in a haunted house.

Charlie Ewan M D (6)

Wellgate Primary School, Mapplewell

Halloween Horrors

Halloween tastes like many scrummy
sour sweets.
Halloween looks like blood drying in a
graveyard where under the ground, zombies
are waking from their dirty creepy coffins.
Halloween sounds like a wolf
howling at the big full moon.
Halloween smells like sticky sweets.
Halloween feels like a creepy spiderweb
spun by a terrifying tarantula.

Betsy Lea (6)
Wellgate Primary School, Mapplewell

Halloween

Halloween smells like sweet zombies.
Halloween sounds like children.
Some children are in costumes.
Halloween feels like an exciting time.
Halloween tastes like candy.
Halloween looks like scary ghosts and spiders.

Noah Michael Taylor (6)
Wellgate Primary School, Mapplewell

Halloween Horrors

Halloween smells like blood and ghosts.
Halloween sounds like ghosts saying, "Ooo!"
Halloween feels like an ugly witch's
cauldron with spiders.
Halloween tastes like gooey blood.
Halloween looks like a creepy ghost
roundabout.

Harris C (6)
Wellgate Primary School, Mapplewell

Autumn

Autumn smells of tasty food.
Autumn tastes like yummy chocolate.
Autumn looks like colourful leaves.
Autumn feels like prickly cones
And crunchy leaves.
Autumn reminds me of fun times.

Gabriella M (5)

Wellgate Primary School, Mapplewell

Horrors

Halloween smells like a scary witch's cauldron.
Halloween sounds like a witch cackling.
Halloween feels like many sticky cobwebs.
Halloween tastes like sticky sweets.
Halloween looks like a vampire's blood.

Sam S (6)

Wellgate Primary School, Mapplewell

Trick Or Treat

Halloween smells like pumpkin pie
that has been cooked in the oven.
Halloween sounds like some wolves
howling in the moonlight.
Halloween feels like a hard skeleton bone.
Halloween tastes like many tasty sweets
from children's bags.
Halloween looks like a few ghosts
flying in the sky.

Sophie E (6)
Wellgate Primary School, Mapplewell

Autumn

Autumn smells of juicy berries
and sour sweeties in my mouth.
Autumn tastes like warm meat in the oven.
Autumn looks like leaves
falling down from the trees.
Autumn feels like cold mornings.
Autumn sounds like crunchy leaves.
Autumn reminds me of birds tweeting
and eating delicious food.

Matilda Rose Hope (5)
Wellgate Primary School, Mapplewell

Halloween

Halloween looks like lanterns glowing.
Halloween smells like juicy candy.
Halloween feels like sticky toffee apples.
Halloween tastes like lots of sticky sweets.
Halloween sounds like werewolves howling.

Riley M (6)
Wellgate Primary School, Mapplewell

Halloween

Halloween looks like the burning lids
of pumpkins.
Halloween smells like toffee apples.
Halloween feels very yummy.
Halloween tastes like a pumpkin pie.
Halloween sounds like spooky noises.

Harry Flintham (6)

Wellgate Primary School, Mapplewell

Halloween

Halloween looks like haunted massive
houses and scary freaky houses.
Halloween smells like burning pumpkins and
scary pumpkins.
Halloween feels like scary massive witches
and spooky ghosts.
Halloween tastes like lovely sweets and
sticky sweets.
Halloween sounds like haunted witches
screaming.

Louie F (6)
Wellgate Primary School, Mapplewell

Autumn

Autumn tastes like nice leaves and bread.
Autumn feels like nice fresh air.
Autumn smells of nice delicious candy.
Autumn sounds like crunchy leaves.
Autumn reminds me of leaves and fresh air.

Tiana S (5)
Wellgate Primary School, Mapplewell

Halloween

Halloween looks like a scary witch stirring a spooky, poisonous potion.
Halloween smells like boiling hot, swirling smoke from a candle.
Halloween feels like super sticky cobwebs.
Halloween tastes like gummy, delicious, sugary gummy sweets.
Halloween sounds like scary werewolves howling.

Charlie Exley (6)
Wellgate Primary School, Mapplewell

Autumn

Autumn smells like sour sweets
in my mouth.
Autumn tastes like yummy chocolate
orange around the campfire.
Autumn looks like a mat of rainbow leaves.
Autumn feels really windy and sunny.
Autumn sounds like rain on my roof.
Autumn reminds me of Halloween
and black cats.

Alanis King (5)
Wellgate Primary School, Mapplewell

Halloween

Halloween tastes like jelly, sticky sweets.
Halloween looks like some people in scary,
colourful costumes trick or treating.
Halloween feels like soft spooky costumes.
Halloween smells like boiling, stinky
cauldrons.
Halloween sounds like some wicked, green
witches laughing loudly.

Violet Valentine Jackson (6)

Wellgate Primary School, Mapplewell

Halloween Horrors

Halloween looks like sticky spiderwebs that spiders have made.
Halloween looks like a haunted village.
Halloween sounds like children saying, "Trick or treat!"
Halloween feels like an exciting thing to do.
Halloween tastes like sticky sweets that children have collected.

Layla Louise Kaye (6)
Wellgate Primary School, Mapplewell

Halloween

Halloween looks like lots of white.
bony skeletons.
Halloween smells like smoky,
roasting pumpkins.
Halloween feels like mouthwatering
chocolate.
Halloween tastes like green, slimy lollies.
Halloween sounds like lots of cackling
witches flying through the air.

Ethan Ogley (6)
Wellgate Primary School, Mapplewell

Halloween

Halloween looks like gruesome zombies.
Halloween looks like scary spiders making shiny cobwebs.
Halloween looks like some yummy candyfloss.
Halloween tastes like yummy sweets.
Halloween sounds like spooky noises.
Halloween smells like sticky chocolate in bags.

Archie J Chapman stott (6)

Wellgate Primary School, Mapplewell

Autumn

Autumn smells of an autumn breeze.
Autumn tastes like purple blueberries.
Autumn looks like red leaves swirling.
Autumn feels cold.
Autumn sounds like a breeze blowing
in the wind.
Autumn reminds me of going to an
exciting bonfire.

Rosie B (5)
Wellgate Primary School, Mapplewell

Autumn

Autumn smells of damp sticks and wet mud.
Autumn feels cold and snowy.
Autumn tastes like tasty hot dogs.
Autumn looks cold and snowy.
Autumn feels like cold wind.
Autumn sounds like crunchy leaves.
Autumn reminds me of my warm coat.

Lewis Cummings (5)
Wellgate Primary School, Mapplewell

Autumn

Autumn smells of sweet tasty
marshmallows.
Autumn tastes like plump blackberries,
juicy and sweet.
Autumn looks like bright, colourful,
red leaves.
Autumn feels like dark chilly mornings.
Autumn sounds like crunching, red leaves.

Luca F Lazzarano (5)

Wellgate Primary School, Mapplewell

Trick Or Treat

Halloween smells like delicious sweets.
Halloween sounds like creepy noises.
Halloween feels like when I get some sweets
and when some spiders are crawling on me.
Halloween tastes like yummy sweets.
Halloween looks very scary.

Brooke Carolyne Seward (6)

Wellgate Primary School, Mapplewell

Autumn

Autumn smells of damp sticks and
smoky fires.
Autumn tastes like sweet toffee.
Autumn looks like colourful leaves.
Autumn feels like chocolate.
Autumn sounds like birds tweeting.
Autumn reminds me of Bonfire Night.

Archie Daniel Mallinder (5)
Wellgate Primary School, Mapplewell

Autumn

Autumn smells of smoky bonfires.
Autumn tastes like good food.
Autumn looks like golden leaves
falling from a tree.
Autumn feels like a warm coat.
Autumn sounds like crunching leaves.
Autumn reminds me of bonfires.

Brooklyn B (5)
Wellgate Primary School, Mapplewell

Halloween Horrors

Halloween smells like sticky sweets.
Halloween sounds like some ghostly noises.
Halloween feels like a nice time and sweet tasty pie.
Halloween tastes like pumpkin.
Halloween looks like lots of fun with scary tarantulas.

Amelia Rachel Galloway (6)
Wellgate Primary School, Mapplewell

Halloween

Halloween looks like spooky pumpkins.
Halloween smells like smelly potions.
Halloween tastes like scary sweets.
Halloween sounds like zombies screaming
and infecting people.
Halloween feels like furry spiders.

Jack C (6)
Wellgate Primary School, Mapplewell

Autumn

Autumn smells of a winter breeze.
Autumn tastes like apples.
Autumn looks like orange leaves.
Autumn feels like a winter breeze.
Autumn sounds like tweeting birds.
Autumn reminds me of jumping in leaves.

Charlotte Buckle (5)
Wellgate Primary School, Mapplewell

Halloween

Halloween looks like monsters
are coming out of the grave.
Halloween smells like some sugary,
spooky sweets.
Halloween feels like spooky spiders on you.
Halloween sounds like wicked witches
laughing.

Chloe Anna Hague (6)
Wellgate Primary School, Mapplewell

Autumn

Autumn smells of crackling bonfires.
Autumn looks like golden brown leaves.
Autumn tastes like hot tasty food.
Autumn sounds like crunchy leaves
on the forest floor.
Autumn reminds me of a dark sky.

Ollie Beau Rawson (5)
Wellgate Primary School, Mapplewell

Autumn

Autumn smells of sweet chocolate.
Autumn tastes like juicy strawberries.
Autumn looks like colourful leaves.
Autumn feels very soft.
Autumn sounds very tinkly.
Autumn reminds me of pretty colours.

Daisy Olivia M (6)
Wellgate Primary School, Mapplewell

Autumn

Autumn smells of smoky bonfires.
Autumn tastes like juicy blackberries.
Autumn looks like furry squirrels.
Autumn feels like crunchy leaves.
Autumn sounds like wind
Blowing in the trees.

Robert W (5)

Wellgate Primary School, Mapplewell

Halloween

Halloween looks like scary monsters.
Halloween smells like burning pumpkins.
Halloween feels like bats.
Halloween tastes like some gummy sweets.
Halloween smells like stinky vampire breath.

Owen S (6)
Wellgate Primary School, Mapplewell

Autumn

Autumn smells of sweet blackberries.
Autumn tastes like juicy blackberries.
Autumn looks like pretty leaves
falling down.
Autumn feels warm and cold.
Autumn reminds me of white snow.

Daisy Mary Knight (5)
Wellgate Primary School, Mapplewell

Autumn

Autumn smells of nice flowers.
Autumn tastes like sugary sweets.
Autumn looks like nice flowers.
Autumn feels cold so I wear warm clothes.
Autumn reminds me of Great Grandad Sid.

Maisie G (5)

Wellgate Primary School, Mapplewell

Autumn

Autumn smells of juicy apples.
Autumn tastes like sweet apples.
Autumn feels like a colourful butterfly.
Autumn sounds like trees blowing.
Autumn reminds me of leaves crunching.

Autumn M (5)
Wellgate Primary School, Mapplewell

Autumn

Autumn smells of damp sticks and wet mud.
Autumn tastes white and warm.
Autumn looks like pretty colourful leaves.
Autumn sounds like leaves.
Autumn reminds me of cold days.

Tommy T (6)
Wellgate Primary School, Mapplewell

Autumn

Autumn smells of smoky bonfires.
Autumn looks like orange leaves.
Autumn tastes like crunchy food.
Autumn sounds like crunchy leaves.
Autumn reminds me of nice flowers.

Kian S (5)
Wellgate Primary School, Mapplewell

Autumn

Autumn smells of chocolate.
Autumn looks like golden brown leaves.
Autumn tastes like hot tasty food.
Autumn sounds like crunchy leaves.
Autumn reminds me of chocolate.

Zain C (5)
Wellgate Primary School, Mapplewell

Autumn

Autumn reminds me of crackling bonfires.
Autumn looks golden brown.
Autumn tastes like tasty food.
Autumn sounds like crunchy leaves.
Autumn reminds me of a dark sky.

Charlie H (5)
Wellgate Primary School, Mapplewell

Autumn

Autumn smells like fresh air.
Autumn tastes like orange leaves.
Autumn looks like orange leaves.
Autumn feels like hard rocks.
Autumn sounds like singing birds.

John S (5)
Wellgate Primary School, Mapplewell

Halloween

Halloween looks like a broomstick.
Halloween smells like roasting pumpkin.
Halloween feels like some stringy
pumpkin seeds.
Halloween tastes like some fun.

Emily S (6)
Wellgate Primary School, Mapplewell

Halloween

Halloween looks like skeletons.
Halloween smells like sweet orange candy.
Halloween tastes like some orange sweets.
Halloween sounds like some grinning devils.

Ashton O (7)
Wellgate Primary School, Mapplewell

Halloween

Halloween smells like some old blood
from a vampire.
Halloween sounds like scary screams.
Halloween feels scary.
Halloween looks like scary zombie blood.

Riley F (6)
Wellgate Primary School, Mapplewell

Autumn

Autumn smells of fresh air.
Autumn tastes like red apples.
Autumn looks like orange leaves.
Autumn feels like hard stones.
Autumn sounds windy.

James V (5)
Wellgate Primary School, Mapplewell

Autumn

Autumn smells of fresh air.
Autumn looks foggy.
Autumn feels like clouds.
Autumn sounds like singing birds.
Autumn reminds me of cold nights.

Harry Jay Thomas (5)
Wellgate Primary School, Mapplewell

Halloween Horrors

Halloween smells like a vampire.
Halloween sounds like a witch.
Halloween feels like some sticky sweets.
Halloween looks like some tasty treats.

Harri Ball (6)

Wellgate Primary School, Mapplewell

Autumn

Autumn smells of sticks.
Autumn tastes like juicy apples.
Autumn looks like trees.
Autumn sounds like birds.
Autumn reminds me of playing.

Lily Littledyke (5)
Wellgate Primary School, Mapplewell

Autumn

Autumn smells like smoky bonfires.
Autumn looks like orange leaves.
Autumn tastes like sweet food.
Autumn sounds like crunchy leaves.

Oliver J (5)
Wellgate Primary School, Mapplewell

Autumn

Autumn smells of smoky bonfires.
Autumn looks like orange leaves.
Autumn tastes like food.
Autumn sounds like crunchy leaves.

Oscar Lumb (5)
Wellgate Primary School, Mapplewell

Autumn

Autumn smells of smoky bonfires.
Autumn looks like smoky leaves.
Autumn tastes like brown food.

Noah E (5)
Wellgate Primary School, Mapplewell